LU & CLANCY'S
SECRET LANGUAGES

written by **Louise Dickson**

illustrated by **Pat Cupples**

Kids Can Press

Kids Can Press acknowledges the financial support of the Ontario Arts Council, the Canada Council for the Arts and the Government of Canada, through the BPIDP, for our publishing activity.

Published in Canada by
Kids Can Press Ltd.
29 Birch Avenue
Toronto, ON M4V 1E2

Published in the U.S. by
Kids Can Press Ltd.
2250 Military Road
Tonawanda, NY 14150

Edited by Valerie Wyatt
Designed by Julia Naimska
Printed in Hong Kong
by Wing King Tong Company Limited

The hardcover edition of this book is smyth sewn caseboard.
The paperback edition of this book is limp sewn with a drawn-on cover.

CM 01 0 9 8 7 6 5 4 3 2 1
CM PA 01 0 9 8 7 6 5 4 3 2 1

Canadian Cataloguing in Publication Data

Dickson, Louise, 1959–
    Lu & Clancy's secret languages

(Lu & Clancy)
1-55337-025-2 (bound)   1-55074-695-2 (pbk.)

1. Ciphers — Juvenile literature. 2. Cryptography — Juvenile literature. I. Cupples, Patricia. II. Title. III. Title: Lu and Clancy's secret languages. IV. Series.

Z103.3.D52 2001   j652'.8   C00-931216-1

Kids Can Press is a Nelvana company

For my parents,
Jim and Lucila Dickson,
with love — LD

For Cleo
and Watson — PC

Contents

furrin' Language

Dog detectives Lu and Clancy stared at the odd pair walking toward them. A large jet-black tomcat wearing a sapphire collar swaggered down the street, while a pudgy little bulldog grunted along at his heels.

Clancy signaled Lu to be quiet. Then he pricked up his ears to hear what the strangers were saying.

"Ru-ru-hu-bies-ries-hies, di-ri-hi-a-ra-ha-monds-ronds-honds, pearls-rearls-hearls," purred the cat.

Clancy scratched his head. The singsong words sounded familiar, but they made no sense.

"They must be talking a furrin' language," whispered Lu.

"Or a *secret* language." Clancy thought for a moment. "I think that cat was speaking the secret language of Ra-Ha."

Secrets of the Ra-Ha

The secret language of Ra-Ha is easy to learn.

1. Say the word or the first syllable of the word. For example, for "doggy," say the first syllable, "dog."

2. Repeat that word or syllable, but replace the first letter or sound with the letter "r." Say "dog-rog."

3. Repeat the word or syllable a second time, but replace the first letter or sound with the letter "h." Say "dog-rog-hog."

4. Repeat steps 1 to 3 with the second syllable, if there is one. Say "gy-ry-hy."

5. Put it all together. So "doggy" becomes "dog-rog-hog-gy-ry-hy." "The doggy chased the cat" would be "The-re-he dog-rog-hog-gy-ry-hy chased-rased-hased the-re-he cat-rat-hat."

Can you figure out what the black cat was saying to the bulldog?
Answer on page 40.

Why-ry-hy won't-ron't-hon't oys-roys-hoys-ters-rers-hers share-rare-hare their-reir-heir pearls-rearls-hearls?

They're-rey're-hey're shell-rell-hell-fish-rish-hish.

> Need help decoding any of the secret languages? Turn to page 40.

Jailhouse Talk

Clancy put his feet up on the couch and clicked on the TV.

"We interrupt our regular programming to bring you this news bulletin," said the stern-faced newscaster. "Leonardo, the slippery and sly master of secret languages, has just been released from prison."

"Lu, come quick!" Clancy shouted. Lu scampered into the room just in time to see a mug shot of the cat with the sapphire collar who had purred past them the day before. She groaned. Both dogs listened closely as the newscast continued.

Piggy Prattle

Clancy was speaking Pig Latin. So can you.

1. If a word begins with a single consonant, move the first letter to the end of the word and add the sound "ay." For example, "get" becomes "et-gay." "Help" becomes "elp-hay."

2. If a word begins with more than one consonant, move the consonant group to the end of the word and add "ay." For example, "school" becomes "ool-schay." "Frog" becomes "og-fray."

"Although Leonardo has served a long sentence for cat burglary, police have never recovered the jewels he stole. Police are hoping Leonardo will try to contact Grump, his former partner in crime, who may have been hiding the loot while Leonardo was in prison. Police are vowing to keep a close eye on Leonardo."

"He may be a master of secret languages," Clancy told Lu, "ut-bay etectives-day ind-fay ecret-say anguages-lay ery-vay useful-way, oo-tay."

"Excuse me?"

3. If a word begins with a vowel, add "way" to the end. For example, "apple" becomes "apple-way." "Orange" becomes "orange-way."

What did Clancy say to Lu?
Answer on page 40.

At-whay o-day ou-yay ive-gay o-tay a-way ore-say ig-pay?

Oinkment-way.

Drawing a Blank

The telephone rang.

"Ello-hay." Sometimes Lu got carried away. "I mean, hello. Lu and Clancy, Dog Detectives."

"Doberman here." Lu recognized the deep rumble of the police detective's voice. "We found a large piece of white paper under the mattress when we were cleaning out Leonardo's jail cell. I want you to have a look at it."

A little later, Detective Doberman arrived with a blank piece of paper.

"If there's anything on it, we'll soon find out," said Lu. She plunged the paper into a bucket of cold water. Like magic, a drawing appeared before their eyes.

Water Magic

You can send and receive invisible messages with the help of wet paper.

You'll need:

- 2 sheets of white paper
- water
- a ballpoint pen

1. Soak one sheet of paper in water and lay it flat on a hard surface such as a kitchen counter.

2. Cover the wet paper with a dry sheet of paper.

3. Write your message on the dry sheet with a ballpoint pen.

4. Throw away the dry sheet of paper and let the wet paper dry. The secret message will disappear. To make it reappear, hold the paper under running water.

Why are fish so smart?

Because they swim in schools.

RasCals' Rendezvous

Detective Doberman studied the drawing that appeared on the paper. Lu and Clancy leaned over his shoulder to get a better look. It seemed to be the inside of a building, and it was covered with strange words.

"Ward-back," Clancy breathed. "It's a secret backward language."

Clancy pointed to the drawing. "Ter-oys — that's oyster! Ga-u-bel — that's beluga! And X marks the spot!" Clancy wagged his tail furiously. "Leonardo is planning to meet someone at the aquarium, right beside the oyster tank."

"We ter-bet get ing-mov," said Lu, catching on.

"You're right, Lu." Clancy turned to Detective Doberman. "Why don't Lu and I go to the aquarium and see what we can find out?"

Back to front

To speak Ward-back, you've got to speak backward.

1. One-syllable words stay the same.

2. For two-syllable words, move the first syllable to the end of the word. For example, "turtle" becomes "tle-tur." "Chicken" becomes "en-chick."

3. For words with more than two syllables, move the last syllable to the beginning of the word and the first syllable to the end. For example, "octopus" becomes "pus-to-oc" and "elephant" becomes "phant-e-el."

Thievesdropping

Lu and Clancy were about to leave for the aquarium when — *beep! beep! beep!* It was Detective Doberman's pager. "Mind if I use your phone?" he asked. "It's the chief — I've got to call him."

After a few minutes, Doberman passed the receiver to Clancy. "We tapped Leonardo's phone. The chief wants you to listen to a message."

Clancy took the receiver and listened to Leonardo's velvety, purring voice.

"The-iggity time-iggity to-iggity meet-iggity
is-iggity half-iggity past-iggity two-iggity.
The-iggity place-iggity is-iggity wet-iggity-
ter-iggity than-iggity the-iggity zoo-iggity."

"It's the aquarium, all right," said Clancy after he hung up. "If my Iggity is as good as I think it is, we have about an hour to get there."

Hot-diggity

Iggity is a very simple language to learn.

1. For one-syllable words, say the word and add "iggity." For example, "phone" becomes "phone-iggity."

2. If the word has two or more syllables, add "iggity" after each syllable. For example, "secret" becomes "se-iggity-cret-iggity."

Can you figure out what Leonardo's message says? Answer on page 40.

How-iggity do-iggity you-iggity write-iggity
to-iggity a-iggity fish-iggity?

Drop-iggity it-iggity a-iggity line-iggity.

Steamy Secrets

Disguised as tourists, Lu and Clancy entered the aquarium. The big, bubbly tanks were a living rainbow of brightly colored fish. There were angelfish, dogfish, starfish, zebra fish and a slinky, slimy octopus hiding behind a rock.

Out of the corner of her eye, Lu saw a furry black tail disappear around a tank.

It was 2:30 P.M. — the meeting time — but no one was waiting by the oyster tank. Clancy stared into a tank and watched a tiny hermit crab scurry sideways across the pebbly bottom. He sighed.

"Clancy, look what you've done," Lu barked excitedly. Word pictures had suddenly appeared on the glass in the fog made by Clancy's breath. "It's a hidden message."

The two dogs started puffing all over the aquarium tank. A little later, wheezing and out of breath, they sat down and surveyed their handiwork.

"Drat. They know we're after them," said Clancy.

Picture Perfect

You can write a message in the steam on your bathroom mirror or window after you've had a bath or shower. The message will disappear as the steam dries, but it will reappear when the next person has a shower. To fool your friends, you can draw your message in pictograms.

1. To create a pictogram, think of a word and see if you can draw a picture

of what the word sounds like. For example, for "I," draw 👁 .

For "can," draw 🥫 .   For "would," draw 🪵 .

2. You can also use letters or numbers for the word itself.
Write "R" for "are," "U" for "you," "4" for "for" and "8" for "ate."

3. Combine letters with pictures for more complicated pictograms.
Write T👂 for "tears."

Can you decode the pictogram that Lu and Clancy found? Answer on page 40.

Words of Warning

Suddenly Lu and Clancy heard screams coming from the gift shop.

"My ring! My diamond ring — it's gone!"

Natalie, the salesclerk, stood crying in the center of the shop, hemmed in by security guards.

Lu wriggled through their legs. "What's up?"

"I was wrapping a gift when somebody with hairy black paws grabbed my wrist and handed me a piece of paper," Natalie sobbed. "I looked down to see what it said. But it was blank. That's when I noticed that my diamond ring was gone." She started to wail again.

Looking for clues, Lu held the piece of paper up to a hot lightbulb.

"I think there's something here." Sure enough, words started to appear on the paper.

Back off, you two, I've done my time,
And soon the treasure will be mine.
I'll give the ring back if you go,
But if you stay, I'll be your foe.
Leo

A Clean Slate

There are lots of ways to make invisible ink. No fancy chemicals are needed — just head into the kitchen and open the fridge.

You'll need:

- a lemon, potato or apple
- a toothpick, cotton swab or fine paintbrush as a writing tool
- paper
- bowl

1. For lemon ink, squeeze the juice of one lemon into a bowl. Dip your writing tool into the lemon juice, then write your secret message on a piece of paper. Let the juice dry completely. To make the message reappear, hold the paper up to a hot lightbulb or radiator.

2. For potato ink, cut a raw potato in half and scoop out the center with a spoon. Some juice will collect in the hole. Dip your writing tool into the potato juice, then write your secret message on a piece of paper. Let the juice dry completely. To make the message reappear, ask an adult to run a warm iron over it.

3. For apple ink, stick a toothpick into a tiny piece of apple and write a secret message by rubbing the apple on the paper. Use a new piece of apple as needed. Let the apple juice dry completely. To make the message reappear, ask an adult to run a warm iron over it.

Why does the ocean roar?

You would, too, if you had crabs in your bed.

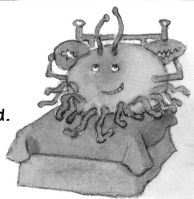

Kooky Conversation

Clancy put his nose to the ground and picked up Leonardo's scent. Snuffling along the floor, he followed the scented trail to a closet marked "Janitor." Angry voices came from behind the door. Clancy stood on his hind legs and put his ear to the keyhole. He strained to hear what was being said.

"Koo-I koo-have koo-been koo-patient koo-long koo-enough," someone hissed. "Koo-get koo-rid koo-of koo-them."

"But, Leo — the treasure's safe," a second voice replied. "I put it in ..."

Where? Where? Clancy pressed harder and harder against the door, struggling to hear. Then suddenly — *blam!* — the door snapped open, and Clancy somersaulted through the air into a pile of brooms and mops.

"Koo-hi," he said into the bucket jammed on his head. When he pulled his head free, Clancy was face to face with Leonardo and Grump.

Get Kooking!

Leonardo and Grump were speaking the secret language of Koo-Koo. You can, too.

Add the sound "koo" before each word. For example, "camera" becomes "koo-camera." "Hide" becomes "koo-hide." "Hide the camera" becomes "Koo-hide koo-the koo-camera."

What was Leonardo saying to Grump? Answer on page 40.

Koo-what koo-did koo-the koo-catfish koo-yell koo-when koo-it koo-got koo-caught koo-in koo-the koo-seaweed?

Koo-kelp!! Koo-kelp!!!

Up in Arms

Clancy had disappeared. Lu was getting frantic. She trotted through the aquarium searching for a sign from her friend — past spiny lump suckers, stiff-looking starfish and frilly anemones. She gasped as she passed a murky tank with a ferocious-looking hammerhead shark.

Tap, tap, tap. Startled, Lu spun around. A slinky, slimy octopus was tapping on the aquarium glass. Was it trying to get her attention?

Lu watched the tips of the octopus's tentacles curling and waving and wiggling through the dark blue water. Sign language!

Lu didn't know which of the eight sucker-lined arms to watch first. *I need a course in speed-reading,* she thought. But with a little concentration, she decoded this message:

"They've got him, Lu.
It's up to you
To save your friend
And the fortune, too.
Something fishy's going on.
I'll keep an eye out for the con."

Fingering It Out

The octopus had borrowed a sign language used by people who are hearing impaired. There is a sign for each letter of the alphabet. With a little practice, you can learn to talk with your hands.

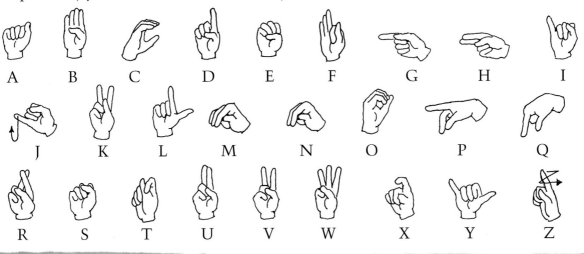

What did the octopus sing to its sweetheart?

I want to hold your hand, hand, hand, hand, hand, hand, hand, hand.

Between the Lies

LEONARDO

The dusky cat loomed over Clancy.

"Start writing," Leonardo commanded with a sinister swish of his tail. "I want your pip-squeak playmate out of my fur. Tell Lu the treasure's at the bottom of Kitty Canal. Tell her you'll meet her there in an hour."

Trembling, Clancy took the pen and wrote the letter as instructed. But when Leonardo wasn't looking, Clancy dipped his pen in the cat's milk saucer and wrote his own invisible message over top of the letter. He scribbled frantically, "Don't be fooled. Stay close. The jewels must be somewhere in the aquarium. Clancy."

"I'll take that." Leonardo clawed the note away from Clancy. "Come on, Grump. Time to play postdog."

The Milky Way

Clancy wrote his message to Lu with milk. He wrote in the spaces between the lines. If you want to be sure a message can't be read, give the page a quarter turn before you start writing your milky message.

You'll need:

- milk
- a saucer
- a toothpick
- newsprint
- ashes, dirt or coffee grounds

1. Pour a little milk into the saucer.

2. Dip a toothpick into the milk and write your message on the newsprint.

3. To make your letter harder to decode, turn the page a quarter turn and write the second half across the lines you've already written. Let your message dry completely.

> Dear Lu,
> I have found the treasure. It is at the bottom of Kitty Canal. Meet me there in one hour.
> Clancy.

4. To make your message appear, lightly rub some ashes, dirt or coffee grounds over it.

What do you get when you cross two elephants with a fish?

Swimming trunks.

Bottle Babble

Clancy was all alone in the cramped janitor's closet. Or was he? Scrabbling sounds on the floor made him jump. Looming shapes in the corner made him cringe. His heart was pounding.

He whistled to keep up his spirits while he found a candle and some matches. *That's better,* he thought as the candlelight turned the ghastly, shadowy creatures into ordinary mops and brooms.

A pair of coveralls, labeled "Grump," hung from a hook on the wall. *So Grump is the aquarium caretaker,* thought Clancy. *This is where he's been hiding all these years.*

On a shelf next to the coveralls, he saw bottles of fish food. One was labeled "Jum-e-wow-e-lob Hub-e-i-sis-tub." He took the jar down and opened it. Instead of fish food, there was a piece of paper. *Hmmmm, what's this?* Clancy pulled it out and started to read.

Tub-wow-e-lob-vum-e o'cab-lob-o-cab-kut
A-tub tub-hub-e lob-o-a-dad-i-non-glug dad-o-cab-kut,
Sis-o bab-rub-i-non-glug a tub-rub-u-cab-kut,
Wow-e'lob-lob bab-e i-non lob-u-cab-kut.

Lob-e-o

Aping the Sounds

Clancy finally figured out that the funny words on the bottle and the piece of paper were written in Gorilla Babble. Here's how to decode the message.

Each letter in Gorilla Babble has its own silly sound. To speak or write Gorilla Babble, spell the word in its new sounds. For example, "Clancy" would be "Cab-lob-a-non-cab-yak." "Lu" would be "Lob-u."

A — a
B — bab
C — cab
D — dad
E — e
F — fob
G — glug

H — hub
I — i
J — jum
K — kut
L — lob
M — mum
N — non

O — o
P — pop
Q — quip
R — rub
S — sis
T — tub
U — u

V — vum
W — wow
X — x
Y — yak
Z — zip

Can you figure out what the label on the bottle said? What about the message inside? Answers on page 40.

Why did the lobster blush?

It saw the salad dressing.

Closetphobia

Where was Lu? How Clancy hated being locked in this tiny closet! He had to get out. He had to get another message to Lu. HE HAD TO GET OUT! He had to calm down. He took a deep breath. He would write another note.

He carefully scraped some soft melted wax from around the candle. He rolled it into the shape of a pencil, then started to write:

"Leonardo and Grump are planning to move the jewels from the aquarium tonight. Clancy. P.S. GET ME OUT OF HERE!!"

Clancy slid the note under the door and hoped someone would find it before Grump came back. He thought he heard squishy sucking noises as something made its way across the floor outside.

White Writing

Clancy wrote a secret message in wax. You can, too.

You'll need:

- a white candle with a pointed end
- scissors
- a piece of white paper
- dirt, chalk or coffee grounds

1. Cut the wick on the candle right down to the wax.

2. Write your message on the paper with the pointed end of the candle.

3. To make your invisible message appear, sprinkle it with dirt, chalk or coffee grounds.

What is the richest fish?

A goldfish.

Undercoveralls

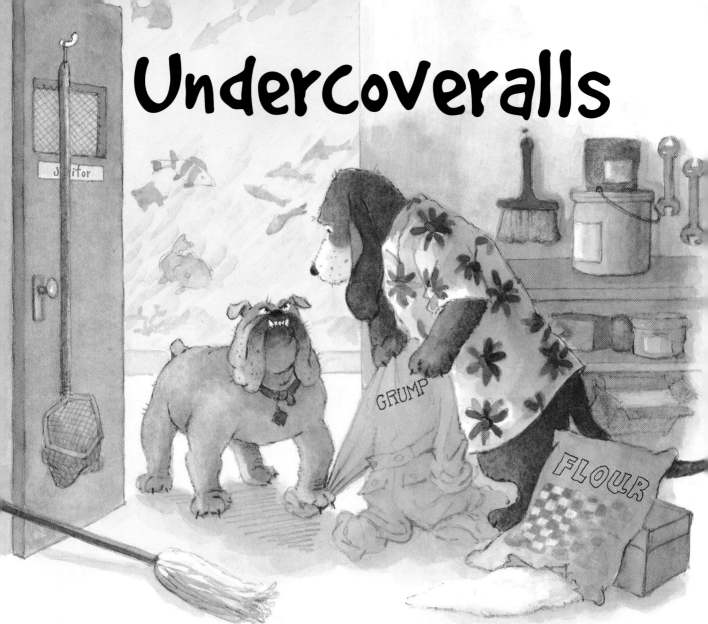

Clancy was really worried. Where was Lu? She must have missed his message, or she would have set him free by now.

The candle was quickly melting to a stub. Before long, he would be plunged into darkness again. He panicked. He had to get a message out! There must be someone who could help him.

Clancy tried tapping out "S.O.S." on the bottom of the tin bucket. No response. He waved a mop past the window at the top of the door. Still nothing. He howled for help. That just got the sea lions barking.

But dog detectives do not give up. Clancy grabbed a sack of flour and Grump's coveralls. He was just finishing his handiwork when Grump opened the door and snarled at him, "Give me those." Grump struggled into the coveralls and left.

Later in the afternoon, as Grump was tossing food into the squid tank, a bad-tempered squid squirted ink all over his back.

The octopus was watching. What was this? A message had appeared on Grump's coveralls. She swam up to the glass to check it out.

"Am in janitor's closet. Help!! C."

All Around the Circle

Clancy used a flour-and-water mixture to write a message on Grump's coveralls. When the squid squirted ink, the message appeared. You can use the same technique to design T-shirts with your own secret symbol. Ask permission before using a T-shirt.

You'll need:
- an empty plastic squeeze bottle
- 250 mL (1 c.) flour
- 150 mL (2/3 c.) water
- newspaper
- a clean T-shirt
- a crayon
- permanent fabric paint
- a paintbrush
- a clean dishcloth or towel
- an iron

1. Put the flour in the plastic squeeze bottle. Add the water. Put the cap on the bottle and shake well.

2. Cover a table with newspaper. Lay the T-shirt on the table. Smooth out the wrinkles. It should be completely flat.

3. Use a crayon to draw a design or write a slogan on the T-shirt. Draw a circle around the design or slogan.

4. Squeeze the flour-and-water mixture out of the bottle along the crayon lines.

5. When the design is completely dry, paint over it but stay inside the circle.

6. Pick off the dried flour to see your symbol or slogan. To set the paint, cover the design with a clean cloth and ask an adult to iron over it.

A Sign of the Crime

Lu looked into Kitty Canal. There were no jewels. She looked around. There was no Clancy. Lu realized she'd been sent on a wild goose chase. "I should have checked that note more carefully," she scolded herself as she hurried back to the aquarium.

Lu headed straight for the octopus tank. Her many-armed friend raised a tentacle to its rubbery mouth, a sign warning Lu to be quiet.

Lu held up an imaginary phone, a secret signal that meant "Have you got a message for me?"

The octopus nodded — "Yes!" — then made sweeping motions with its arms. "Broom?" asked Lu. She looked around and saw the janitor's closet. The octopus nodded again.

Lu held an imaginary camera up to her eye — "I get the picture."

The octopus gave her the thumbs up — "Good work! Get going."

Body Language

Lu and the octopus were able to speak to each other without saying a word by using secret eye and hand signals. You and your friends can make up your own secret signals and handshakes. Here are a few to get you started.

 Index finger on mouth — "Don't tell anyone."

 Pull left ear — "Careful, spy in area."

 Pull right ear — "I have a message for you."

 Hand on chin — "Wait until dark."

 Hand in pocket — "Take the short cut."

 Scratch neck — "Look casual."

 Tap finger on nose — "Look behind you."

 Point to watch — "Meet me in five minutes."

 Wink right eye — "See you after class."

 Wink left eye — "The coast is clear."

 Blink both eyes — "Abandon operation. Retreat."

Did you hear about the fish who worked as a stand-up comedian?

He was reel funny.

Liberty Lu

Clancy heard a key turning in the lock. His heart sank. It must be the bad guys again. He whimpered and put the bucket over his head.

"Clancy? Is that you?" It was Lu!

The bucket clattered to the ground as Clancy ran around in circles, chasing his tail. It felt great to be free. With a joyful bark, he leaped over Lu. "Follow me," he yelped and raced through the aquarium toward the loading dock.

B-ware

Grump and Leonardo were speaking the secret language of B. Here's how.

1. Say the word or first syllable of the word. For example, for "Monday," say "Mon." Repeat the word or syllable, but replace the first letter or sound with the letter "b." Say "Mon-bon." Say the second syllable, then replace its first letter or sound with the letter "b." Say "day-bay." Put it all together. "Monday" is "Mon-bon-day-bay."

A cold wind blew clouds across the moon. All was silent. Then Lu and Clancy heard a big truck rumbling in the distance. Bright headlights swept through the parking lot. The two dogs hid in the shadows. Clancy heard the truck door open. Grump jumped down from the driver's seat.

"Boss-boss, hur-bur-ry-by. Clan-ban-cy-by has-bas es-bes-caped-baped. We're-be're run-bun-ning-bing out-bout of-bof time-bime," he called to Leo, who was waiting on the loading dock.

The cat yowled in anger. "You-bou fool-bool. You-bou can't-ban't trust-bust a-ba dog-bog to-bo do-bo a-ba cat's-bat's work-bork."

Turn-burn the-be page-bage to-bo see-be what-bat hap-bap-pens-bens next-bext.

2. If a word starts with a vowel, just add "b" when you repeat that word or syllable. For example, "apple" becomes "ap-bap-ple-ble." "Ogre" becomes "o-bo-gre-bre."

Can you figure out what Grump and Leonardo were saying? Answer on page 40.

Tickling Tentacles

On tiptoe, Lu and Clancy followed Leonardo and Grump past the eerily lit tanks of the aquarium. Fish swam up to ogle the shadowy pair tailing the thieves.

"Clancy, I can't see them anymore," Lu whispered. "They've disappeared."

"We need backup," said Clancy. "I'll phone Detective Doberman. Stay here until I get back."

Trying to make herself invisible, Lu pressed her back against one of the tanks. Suddenly, she jumped and stifled a scream. *Oh help!* she thought. There was something on her back!

Too afraid to turn around, she glanced out of the corner of one eye. It was a tentacle. Was the octopus trying to signal her? She felt a damp tentacle start to trace letters on her back as Clancy returned.

"Hey, Clancy, our friend has a message for us." Slowly Lu spelled the letters out loud: "O-Y-S-T-E-R-S."

"Of course!" said Clancy. "Oysters! Come on, Lu. Doberman's on his way."

Writing Back Words

The octopus wrote a message by spelling it out on Lu's back. Try it yourself and see who gets the most words right.

For shorter messages, such as "yes," "no," or "maybe," just tap on your friend's back:

one tap means "no";

two taps mean "yes";

three taps mean "maybe."

Why did the dolphin feel blue?

Its life had no porpoise.

The Shell Out

There they were! Lu, Clancy and Detective Doberman watched Leonardo and Grump take oysters out of the tank and toss them into a big gunnysack.

On cue, the three crime fighters surrounded the thieves.

"The pizza has landed," Clancy said as he handcuffed Leonardo.

"The moon is blue." Lu wrestled Grump to the ground.

Detective Doberman radioed the station, "Chief, do you read me?"

"Ten-four, Doberman. Go ahead."

"We've got a couple of bad apples here. I'm picking them off and wrapping them," barked Doberman.

"Flying pizzas? Blue moons? Huh?" growled Grump.

"Aw, clam up. Our goose is cooked," the cat snapped.

A Code in the Knows

The pizza has landed? The moon is blue? Clancy and Lu were talking in their own secret code. Detective Doberman was speaking police jargon. You and your friends can talk to one another without letting anyone else know what you're saying. Just make up words or phrases that have special meanings for you.

For example:

"I'm doing my homework" could mean "I'm watching TV."

"See you in class" could mean "I'll meet you at the mall."

"Bring a dictionary" could mean "Bring your CDs."

"Let's do laundry" could mean "Let's just hang out."

"I'm shaking the chicken" could mean "I'm having scrambled eggs."

"I'm peeling carrots" could mean "I'm eating a bag of cookies."

"I'm going to the store" could mean "Let's meet at the park."

"I'm raking leaves" could mean "Let's go to a movie."

I'm peeling carrots.

What fish sings in the lowest voice?

A bass.

An Eggciting End

Detective Doberman was worried. "I can't keep those two in custody unless I find the jewels."

"Why, they're right under our noses," said Clancy, peering into the gunnysack. He noticed a bottle of oyster food in the bottom of the sack. He picked it up and stared at the label.

"M-egg-ak-egg-e th-egg-e egg-oyst-egg-ers egg-op-egg-en w-egg-id-egg-e: y-egg-o-egg-u'll b-egg-e s-egg-urpr-egg-is-egg-ed egg-at wh-egg-at's egg-ins-egg-id-egg-e."

"Aha!" said Clancy. "The secret language of Egg." He knew just what to do.

He poured the oyster food into the tank. As the food rained down, the oyster shells began to open. In seconds, the tank was transformed into a sparkling jewel case. The oysters were decked out in the stolen jewels. One was even wearing Natalie's diamond ring.

"Well done, Lu and Clancy," Doberman declared. "Dazzling detective work again."

"It's just dogged determination," quipped Clancy.

"We didn't want to end up with egg on our faces," Lu chortled.

Get Cracking

The instructions on the oyster food were written in the secret language of Egg. It's simple to speak or write Egg.

Put "egg" in front of every vowel. For example, "mother" would be "m-egg-oth-egg-er." "Father" would be "f-egg-ath-egg-er."

Can you figure out what the instructions on the oyster food said?
Answer on page 40.

Wh-egg-at d-egg-id C-egg-in-d-egg-er-egg-ell-egg-a S-egg-e-egg-al w-egg-e-egg-ar t-egg-o th-egg-e b-egg-all?

Gl-egg-ass fl-egg-ipp-egg-ers.

Answers

Furrin' Language,
pages 4–5
The cat says: "Rubies,
diamonds, pearls."

Joke:
Why won't oysters share
their pearls?
They're shellfish.

Jailhouse Talk,
pages 6–7
Clancy says: "But
detectives find secret
languages very useful, too."

Joke:
What do you give to
a sore pig?
Oinkment.

Rascals' Rendezvous,
pages 10–11
Lu says: "We better get
moving."

Thievesdropping,
pages 12–13
Leonardo's message says:
"The time to meet is half
past two. The place is
wetter than the zoo."

Joke:
How do you write
to a fish?
Drop it a line.

Steamy Secrets,
pages 14–15
The pictogram says:
"I saw the dogs.
They're on our tail.
Escape if you can,
Or I'll see you in jail."

Kooky Conversation,
pages 18–19
Leonardo says to Grump:
"I have been patient long
enough. Get rid of them."

Joke:
What did the catfish
yell when it got caught
in the seaweed?
Kelp! Kelp!

Bottle Babble,
pages 24–25
The label on the bottle
says: "Jewel heist."

The message in the
bottle says:
"Twelve o'clock
At the loading dock,
So bring a truck,
We'll be in luck.
Leo"

Liberty Lu,
pages 32–33
Grump says: "Boss, hurry.
Clancy has escaped. We're
running out of time."

Leonardo replies: "You
fool. You can't trust a dog
to do a cat's work."

An Eggciting End,
pages 38–39
The instructions on the
oyster food say: "Make the
oysters open wide: you'll
be surprised at what's
inside."

Joke:
What did Cinderella Seal
wear to the ball?
Glass flippers.